Network Marketing

A Beginner's Guide for a Successful Network Marketing Business.

© Copyright 2017 Connection Books Club
All Rights Reserved.

This document is presented with the desire to provide reliable, quality information about the topic in question and the facts discussed within. This Book is sold under the assumption that neither the publisher or the author should be asked to provide the services discussed within. If any discussion, professional or legal, is otherwise required a proper professional should be consulted.

The reproduction, duplication or transmission of any of the included information is considered illegal whether done in print or electronically. Creating a recorded copy or a secondary copy of this work is also prohibited unless the action of doing so is first cleared through the Publisher and condoned in writing. All rights reserved.

Any information contained in the following pages is considered accurate and truthful and that any liability through inattention or by any use or misuse of the topics discussed within falls solely on the reader. There are no cases in which the Publisher of this work can be held responsible or be asked to provide reparations for any loss of monetary gain or other damages which may be caused by following the presented information in any way shape or form.

The following information is presented purely for informative purposes and is therefore considered universal. The information presented within is done so without a contract or any other type of assurance as to its quality or validity.

Any trademarks which are used are done so without consent and any use of the same does not imply consent or permission was gained from the owner. Any trademarks or brands found within are purely used for clarification purposes and no owners are in anyway affiliated with this work.

Table of Contents

Introduction 1
The Basic Psychology of Network Marketing 5
Opportunities vs. Scams 18
Product Promotion and Advertisement 25
People Management and Team Building 31
Finding Motivation and Making the Final Sale 37
Communication is Key 40
Keeping Your Eyes on the Competition 46
Building a Steady Income 48
Understanding Taxes.. 51
The Importance of Mentors... 57
Let's Get Started! 59
Conclusion... 66

Introduction

I want to thank you and congratulate you for downloading the book, Network Marketing: A Beginner's Guide for a Successful Network Marketing Career

Network marketing is one of the oldest and most efficient modern methods of making money at home. Many people dream of owning their own business and working for themselves on their own time. Everyone wants the opportunity to have enough time to spend with their loved ones and to do the things they most enjoy. However, very few people realize that the chance to make their dreams come true is right before their eyes!

If you hate going to your nine-to-five job and punching someone else's clock, then you should seriously consider looking into network marketing as a change in career. Every day, more and more people are finding that network marketing is the perfect opportunity to make some extra money while still working a day job. But the most successful network marketers are able to efficiently make their marketing career their only source of income. Network marketing can give you the freedom to live out your dreams by granting you personal freedom with your time and financial independence.

This book contains proven steps and strategies on how to successfully start a career in network marketing, as well as how to choose the right company for your needs and aspirations. You will also learn crucial communication skills and selling techniques that are guaranteed to help you establish and build strong relationships with clients, which in turn will help you make huge sales and improve your business.

Here's an inescapable fact: forcing yourself to go to the same job every day even though it makes you miserable to no end will leave you unfulfilled and discouraged. You finally have the chance to become financially independent and self-sufficient. And fortunately for you, a great deal of the information you need to change your life is right here at your fingertips. It is time for you to take your life and your income into your own hands. You do not have to rely on your boss to sign your paycheck. You have the power to choose a career that will pay you for all of the hard work you put in, and see your own business take off.

Thanks again for downloading this book! Continue reading to learn everything you need to know about building a successful network marketing business. Good luck, and enjoy!

Thank you for your purchase of this eBook! I hope you enjoy reading this eBook as much as I enjoyed writing it. As part of your purchase, I invite you to join my email subscribers. This FREE subscription lets you receive a newsletter, highlighting the great new books available from Connection Books Club and other exclusive business and self development information. Subscribing is easy, and members receive great deals and fantastic eBooks at a discount! All you need to do is click this link to enter your email:

http://www.connectionbooksclub.com/bonus/

In addition to this great opportunity to subscribe to incredible discounts and our newsletter, as a welcome gift, you'll receive a FREE eBook download! Learn how to secure your financial future with the informative eBook, Money Management: Learn How to Organize Your Financial Life and Invest in Your Future. It's yours for FREE once you've enrolled! http://www.connectionbooksclub.com/bonus/

Welcome to the club, and we hope you enjoy your purchase as well as our FREE welcome gift!

Have you ever wished that you were better with money?

Do you ever find yourself being overwhelmed by the state of your personal finances?

Would you like to become more financially responsible?

Now you can, with **5 Reasons to Invest in Money Management: Learn How to Organize Your Financial**

Life and Invest in Your Future, a short self-help book that is packed with information on how to make the most of your financial situation.

If you want to be able to lower your interest rates, learn up to date money management strategies and turn your financial situation into one of prosperity and stability, then you'll find the answers inside, with solid advice that includes:

Strategies which are designed for the average person

Your options for retirement

Hacks for navigating the grocery store's subtle spending traps

Ways to pay less than you owe on credit cards and other outstanding debts

Finding freedom with financial stability

Suitable for complete novices, **5 Reasons to Invest in Money Management** is a book that will transform the way you look at and deal with your finances.

Download a free copy and start investing in your future today! http://www.connectionbooksclub.com/bonus/

Prosperity is waiting for **YOU**!

The Basic Psychology Of Network Marketing

The Basics of Network Marketing

What do companies such as Avon, Sensi, Tupperware, and Mary Kay have in common? In short, they all function off the business plan of network marketing. Network marketing is one of the oldest and most practical methods of selling products and services. Today, many large enterprises use the internet and television to reach potential customers. What makes network marketing different from typical commerce tactics is that companies rely on your personal connections to sell products. Because even though the internet allows companies to reach billions of people around the world, word of mouth is still the most efficient form of advertisement. Your family and friends are more likely to make a purchase if you personally recommend it for them; because they know and trust you.

Network marketing in its simplest definition is a method of marketing products by employing independent representatives to influence potential customers that the company would otherwise not be able to reach through traditional marketing methods. Rather than retaining a few hundred employees on a daily basis, companies are able to utilize people all over the world to sell their products. Network marketing companies are appealing because they feature a low upfront investment, and the chance to sell products directly to personal contacts. While the initial investment covers the cost of a product sample kit, the opportunity to sell any amount of the product can help you make thousands of dollars.

Many consider network marketing as the ideal starting point for becoming financially independent, starting their own business, and creating the foundations for an income. As a company representative, you are able to set your own hours, rather than clocking in for your boss every morning from nine to five. While you may initially believe that network marketing companies are only served by desperate door-to-door salesmen, many of the recruited individuals have grown their branch of the company into a profitable business of their very own.

Have you ever seen a commercial for the insurance industry that advertises the assistance of an independent insurance agent or associate? At first glance, the commercial may appear to be employees of the company, when in reality they are independent business owners taking advantage of their resources. There are many advertisements placed around your neighborhood by these independent marketers designed to capture your attention.

Network marketing companies are well represented, even though you do not always recognize the members of their sales teams. In fact, more than thirteen million people are either directly involved in the network marketing industry or with direct selling. The difference between direct selling and network marketing is that direct selling will limit the representative to an exclusive territory, so that they cannot market outside of that assigned area. But network marketing allows you to work anywhere in the world with anyone you choose, as long as the company you work for is established.

So why exactly are multi-million-dollar companies willing to pay you to sell their products? There are dozens of internet and traditional marketing methods that make it easy for companies to reach millions of customers around the world. Companies spend millions of dollars a year on paying high-priced advertisers to market their products and services. So what makes *you* the ideal candidate for their sales team? Your personal network! The access to your inner circle of friends and family members is the exact connection they need to maximize their profit and help you earn a few extra bucks as well. Word of mouth is a powerful tool in any industry. Companies that thrive on network marketing are more than willing to pay for you to communicate how amazing their products and services are to anyone and everyone you know. Plus, as an insider, you gain access to their products and services, most of which you can recognize by their brand name. Some of the most popular marketing services today cover every industry you can think of, including weight loss programs, internet access, financial programs, solar power, communication services, and nutritional products, just to name a few examples.

Network marketing has gotten a bad rep, as sales representatives are often portrayed as annoying, desperate company puppets. But the business is much more than soliciting your social network to make a few sales. Network marketing is not about bugging your friends and family members in order to force them to buy your merchandise. Network marketing is utilizing your ability and skill to decide who within your inner circle would be interested in the goods and services your business offers. Developing these social skills is crucial to success in this field. This information in itself is one of the most critical factors that determine who will fail and who will become successful in network marketing.

Becoming the Ideal Salesman

Networking is all about interacting with the people around you to establish personal connections that will help establish and build your business. You sell your product by selling yourself with various social networking tactics, inspired by informational and honest conversation about your goods and services. You will never find a somber Avon representative or frowning Tupperware employee, because good salesmen know that a potential customer will not make a purchase from an unhappy representative who does not believe in their own company.

To become a truly experienced network marketer, you need more than just intellect to make a sale. Selling and buying products are mental and psychological exercises. Customers are emotional human beings, not robots who only focus on facts and logic. This is why expert salespeople are masters at controlling their emotions. Every great sales representative has a particular set of skills and personality traits that set them apart from the rest. They are able to use these elements to successfully direct and control conversations with customers and make huge sales.

Assertiveness

> Being assertive does not mean acting like a desperate used car salesman who does not take 'no' for an answer. Unfortunately, this has become the universal image for network markers; but a representative who

expresses this trait is often misunderstood. Assertiveness allows the marketer to push the sales situation forward while avoiding offending or angering the client. Keep in mind that assertiveness is not the same as aggressiveness; your job as a network marketer is not to annoy and badger your family and friends into making a pity purchase. Think of assertiveness as a trait located between belligerence and passivity. Here are three responses that demonstrate the difference between the three:

> *Aggressive:* "If you do not purchase this item right now, then the offer is no longer on the table."
>
> *Assertive:* "Can you give me a specific time when you will be able to make your final decision on this product?"
>
> *Passive:* "You can just call me when you make a decision, there's no rush."

Passive responses will give the potential customer the power and puts the sale on hold indefinitely. You always want to be able to contact the client and feel comfortable doing so in order to make the sale. Definite answers will keep you from wasting your time and avoid making strained relationships. Aggressive responses, on the other hand, will put too much pressure on the customer and make them resent you to the point that they will avoid all future contact with you. This is how the misunderstood idea of the pushy salesman has come to be. An assertive approach will allow you to stay in control of the sale without forcing your customer to change their pace.

Self-Awareness

Your emotions play a crucial role in making sales and being a positive image in representing your company. To be a great salesperson, you must be able to identify your emotions, understand how they affect you, and learn to utilize them in order to strengthen customer relationships. You will never make a sale if you do not keep your emotions in check. Anger that has festered from a fight with your significant other, annoyance at the customer's lack of understanding, and worry about getting to the grocery store before dinner are just a few examples of how your emotions can get the better of you and end up ruining a sale. This four-step method of self- evaluation will help you gain a sense of self-awareness and prepare you for your next sales pitch:

1. Identify your emotions at that point in time. Recognizing how you are feeling is the first step to centering your mindset and overcoming your mental state. Is there anything that is bothering you? Are you worried, scared, angry, happy, relieved?

2. Based on past experiences, take a moment to predict how your current feelings will impact your sales effort. In the past, have your emotions gotten the better of you and hurt your sales pitch? Did they distract you from your sale effort? Or did they

make you more appealing and relatable to the customer?

3. If you are experiencing negative emotions, compensate for them so they do not prevent you from making a sale. The best self-development gurus around the world insist that if you act a certain way, you will adopt that trait. For example, pretending to be happy or excited will actually make you happy and excited. It is also a proven fact that making yourself smile and laugh will lighten your mood and make you feel better. So, whenever you are upset or emotionally unsettled before talking to a client, readjust your feelings and compensate for the bad with the good.

4. Engage in your positive emotions that will make you the sale. It's true what they say: you will get back the energy that you put out into the universe. This means that if you put out positive, happy vibrations, that energy will come back to you. You will not receive a warm smile and welcoming conversation from a customer when you engage with them with a frown on your face. Whatever positive emotions you are feeling, expand them and use them to propel your sale.

If you find yourself unable to let go of any negative emotions, then take a break before engaging in a conversation with your customer. Try reciting positive affirmations, watching a funny video on YouTube, or calling a friend to vent about your day to get rid of any negativity that may be clouding your mental state.

Empathy

> Sympathy is when you understand and pity someone else's situation or feelings. Empathy is when you actually put yourself in their shoes and imagine how they are really feeling based on your own similar experiences. To truly experience empathy, adapt your behavior to your client's emotions. Start by listening to the client and observing their actions. Ask how they are doing and empathize with what they say by feeling what the customer may be feeling – as long as relating to their feelings and adapting the conversation to their mood does not interfere with you making a sale or lead to misrepresenting your company.

Problem Solving

> If you have ever worked in retail or sales before, then you know that the saying 'the customer is always right' is complete garbage. However, if there is a problem that you know you have the power to fix, then it is your job to solve that problem for your client. The customer is putting their faith and trust in you – that is the whole point of accessing your inner circle to excel in network marketing. This does not mean catering to whatever whim amuses them, but meeting them halfway financially and emotionally to prove to the customer that you are reputable and reliable. Problem solving in network marketing needs to be done in a precise and professional manner through this four-step process:
>
> 1. Come to fully understand the problem before attempting to solve it. Let the customer finish

explaining their issue and assess the situation before diving into it.

2. Do not attempt to solve the customer's problem before you fully understand it. See the circumstance as it really is, as some clients tend to exaggerate issues or there may be another side to the story.

3. If the problem at hand is not presenting a favorable outcome for your client, then help them visualize a more ideal situation. What do they really want out of the situation or offer? What were they expecting that did not occur? Once you understand their expectations, you can work to make them happen (within reason, of course).

4. Once you have formulated a plan of action to satisfy the client, communicate that solution in a manner that helps your client come to a decision. Whether the customer wants to make a purchase or not, as a network marketer, you have to help them come to that conclusion. You do not want a sales deal to become stagnant with indecisiveness. So take action and create a resolution.

While this process may seem relatively obvious, there are enough salesmen who practice the exact opposite tactics. They do not invest in their customer's experience and lose sales and clients because of it.

Optimism

If you do not believe that you will sell your product, then you will not make any sales. Tony Robbins once said that pessimists are realists while optimists are dreamers; but optimists also tend to reach higher and succeed with their goals, while pessimists will make less progress and settle. When things go bad during a sales pitch, or you just had a bad day in general, a sense of optimism will help you maintain emotional balance. A sense of optimism also keeps you from being thrown off if one sales effort goes awry. If your first sales call of the day goes wrong, then your performance with every other client has the potential to be affected. Keep your mind focused on the present and optimistic about the outcome of each sales effort, then your day will be filled with positive results and your attitude unhindered. Remember that every sales pitch is different; so if the first one goes bad, then the next one will be much better. There are dozens of opportunities to make sales and become an even better salesman.

The Traits of a Great Salesman

- Caring about the client's interests
- Being Confident
- Always being on your game
- Being open and extroverted
- Listening to your client's needs
- Forming great multitasking skills

- Leading by example
- Engaging every situation with a positive attitude
- Remaining focused and in the present
- Staying organized
- Utilizing existing relationships to make sales
- Knowing your product
- Finding ways to go the extra mile
- Taking initiative
- Willing to learn from mentors and peers
- Staying passionate about your products and services
- Great time management skills
- Is relatable to clients

Practice Makes Perfect

1. Reciting positive affirmations

    One of the worst ways to ruin a sales pitch is psyching yourself out before ever making contact with a client. Your day should be filled with positive affirmations and self-assurance that you are more than capable of achieving your goals and making sales. Practice controlling your inner dialog by using affirmations that are phrased in the present, personal, and optimistic tense.

    - I can do this!
    - I feel great!

- I am a great salesman!
- I know I will make this sale!
- I may not have sold a product to this person, but I will definitely make the next one!

We can control our emotions and the outcome of situations by keeping ourselves in a positive mindset. If you do not consciously try to keep yourself in a positive and optimistic state of mind, then your worry and anxiety will manifest into reality and your potential sales will suffer.

1. Using Positive Visualizations to Manifest Your Goals

    One of the useful abilities is being able to visualize your goals as something that you have already achieved. Close your eyes and envision a clear and inspiring picture of your goal and ideal life to keep you motivated and working hard. Replay this image in your mind until you begin to see these goals manifest into your reality.

2. Surround Yourself with Positive People

    The people you spend the most time with affect who you are and the personality traits you develop. Your friend's or family member's mood can influence yours in a negative way. Try watching YouTube videos and listening to podcasts by successful and motivational people: like Tony Robbins, Zig Ziglar, or Les Brown. These businessmen know what it takes to become a powerful force in the sales world, as well as the skills needed to influence people to believe in you and your product.

A career in network marketing is the stepping stone to personal success. It allows you to call the shots in your own life and learn what it takes to run a successful micro business. If you are willing to learn everything you can about making money by selling useful high-end products, and genuinely enjoy talking and working with people, then network marketing may be the perfect business opportunity for you. However, if you are only involved with this business for the money or are the opposite of a people person, then you will most likely end up failing. Network marketing can be a really rewarding job. It gives you the freedom to choose your own hours and hold yourself accountable for how much money you make. The possibilities in network marketing are endless, giving you the freedom to sell high-quality products while having enough time to do the things you enjoy. You will develop a deeper appreciation for all of the responsibilities that your boss has to handle on a daily basis, as well as invaluable communication skills. Network marketing is a chance for you to take control of your life and make money doing something you love.

Opportunities Vs. Scams

Another stigma that has affected network marketing recruiting is that the business is full of scams and people trying to take your money. The business can get really sticky when a company is more focused on hiring new recruits than selling the actual product or service. In this case, the network marketing company in question would be considered an illegal pyramid scheme. However, there are dozens of network marketing opportunities out there; so how do you know if a company is legitimate? The reason there are so many fraudulent companies out there is because network marketing enterprises are normally exempt from business opportunity regulation, and therefore are not classified as franchises under federal and state franchise laws. There are a number of signs that may give hint as to whether you can trust a marketing company. The following indicators are tell-tale signals that a business is not worth you investing your time and money.

Network marketing scams seem ideal on paper because they feature get-rich-quick self-employment opportunities that allow you to run your own business. But these are just eye-catching features designed to lure you into paying up-front fees and finding other new people to join. Here's how to avoid falling victim to such scams and finding real business opportunities:

1. Do not plan on making money by recruiting other sales representatives

    An entire company based on how many members you can get to join is one of the biggest multi-level marketing scams you can find. When the majority of the income you earn is from finding new members and getting them to join the program, it is known as a pyramid scheme. What makes a pyramid scheme seem so appealing is that you could potentially make an endless amount of money, all you need to earn an income is a few new recruitments. However, pyramid schemes are illegal and should be avoided at all costs.

2. Do not pay to be a part of a business opportunity

    Unfortunately, there is a common saying in the business world that is designed to convince you to invest in whatever business opportunity comes your way: "it takes money to make money." However, forming your own network marketing side-business should not take hundreds of dollars out of your pocket. Any business that requires you to pay a membership fee or purchase a significant amount of their inventory before starting your own branch of the company is a scam. Not only does this scam thrive on your bank account, but also the wallets of anyone else you get to join. A legitimate company will work to meet the needs of the customers and only ask that you pay marketing and operational costs. This could mean purchasing a sample kit of whatever goods you will be selling; in which case, it is more than fair that you pay for the products you will be using to make sales. Membership fees for the privilege of starting up your own business is not normal. If you are being asked to pay multiple unnecessary fees, then this great opportunity is probably a scam.

3. Ask Difficult Questions

   The most dangerous scams are the ones that seem like they provide an explanation to the simplest questions, so that you do not end up asking the members anything that may expose their illegal activity. There are a number of questions that you can ask to identify a scam and keep your bank account safe.

   - Did a member make contact with you to inform you about the actual value and need for his or her product, or for the opportunity to make money?
   - Is the product likely to successfully sell based on its qualities? Or does the product or service have to go through a multi-level marketing distribution system?
   - Does the network marketing company focus on quality products that add value to the customer's life, or does it use trends and good timing, or special or secret formulas to sell their products?
   - As a sales representative, can you make a significant income based on the time you spend selling the goods and services without having to recruit a new person to join the company?
   - Would other distributors who hold a higher position than you be compensated with a payout with each sale you make, regardless of whether or not they were involved in making the sale?
   - Are the prices of the products or services still competitive with similar products and services available through other sources? Does the

- company offer products that are inexpensive enough to make sales, but respectable enough for you to make money by selling it?
- Has the person who is attempting to recruit you been devious or forward about his or her attempts in getting you to join the company?
- Will you be compensated with free training programs, videos, conferences, and classes to prepare you for work? Or are you expected to pay for your training yourself, so that the company can make even more money?

Even with these careful questions, it can still be difficult to decipher which network marketing opportunities are legitimate, and which ones are scams. These false business fronts have been around for decades, and have evolved into carefully planned schemes that seem impossible to expose. As more companies pop up on the internet, and new ways of communication come into play, there are very few times when you can immediately tell that a business is really a scam. And with so many people looking for opportunities to work from home and become self-sufficient, most optimistic aspiring entrepreneurs will overlook many tell-tale signs that signal a bad business opportunity. If you cannot find the answers to the questions listed above, or are still unsure if a network marketing company is right for you, use the following criteria to help confirm your suspicions.

1. The company focuses more on recruiting members than selling their product…

    The most prominent feature of a pyramid scheme is when members are required to recruit a certain number of people to join in order to get paid. A red flag that will quickly indicate a pyramid scheme is if a member is trying to recruit you to join the team, rather than attempting to sell you their product. Does it seem like the company is more focused on "building the sales team" than marketing the actual product? If it seems like recruits are the company's target customers, then you are most likely being pursued by a pyramid scheme.

2. If the company does not take the time to train you properly…

Why would a company not put a significant amount of time and effort into making sure their business is represented by the most efficient, successful, and informed team members? Because the product is not what brings in the money: new recruits are. If a network marketing company is offering you a chance to work for them, ask about the training they provide and the support you receive. If the team members are avoiding directly answering your questions, then you may be falling victim to a multi-level marketing scam. Does the company offer free training seminars and an employee support office to help solve any future issues once you start working? If the training phase does not focus on teaching you how to sell the product or you are required to pay for training, then this may be a scam.

3. If the company is pressuring, you to pay more money after you have joined…

Are higher-up team members pressuring you to invest more money into purchasing more of their products? Are you being asked to join a "fast track" or "elite" employee system that will help you buy a greater amount of inventory all at once, rather than paying for whatever products you need as you go? A real network marketing company is focused more on successfully selling the stock you already have, rather than having an endless supply of goods that are going unused and risk being sent back to storage. Any pressure to "invest" in better sales training or basic supplies is a sign that you may be in trouble with a scam. This is especially crucial to keep in mind when the company offers to help you out by putting your costs on a credit card, rather than only taking cash. They may try to convince you by assuring you that this is a business investment that will pay off in the end.

4. The network marketing opportunity seems too good to be true…

Unfortunately, there are only a handful of businesses in the entire world that have pure intentions and honest opportunities. So, if you find yourself looking at a job ad for a network marketer, or in a conversation with an employee of such a company, then ask yourself "is this too good to be true?" Are the representatives of the company attempting to convince you to join by praising the opportunity and talking about the "amazing" program, without having proof or enough information to back up their claims?

If it seems too good to be true, then it is almost definitely a scam.

Enjoying your eBook so far? Take a moment to subscribe to our FREE newsletter for incredible discounts, books giveaways, and VIP offers!

> http://www.connectionbooksclub.com/bonus/

All we need is your email, and you'll be set up to receive more of the eBooks you can't wait to read.

Product Promotion And Advertisement

Congratulations, you have found a legitimate business opportunity that will make you money while working at home! This exciting chance to be a successful small business owner has finally come around and you can now make a significant income by doing something you love. But just like with any other job, only hard work and dedication will make you money. You have to put in the time and effort to earn a stable income. Just because you can sit at home and enjoy more family time and independence does not mean that you are on a permanent vacation. You have to hit the ground running and start your new business off with a bang!

Network marketing is all about interacting with customers and promoting your product. You have to show real interpersonal skills and an extroverted personality to be successful in this business. You will only be as successful as your advertisements allow you to be. So how do you successfully advertise new, unheard-of products and services and still make max profit? In this age of new media, the internet, and mixture of traditional information outlets, there are dozens of ways to reach out to consumers. By access to both new age and traditional sales channels, you can sell mass amounts of products and find success in your new business venture. Here's how:

- Host Personal Events – Become a Relatable Personality

    Regularly hosting events in your home and asking friends to host events for you are great methods for selling products and services. There are many jewelry, candle, and wine companies that thrive off of hosting parties in customers' homes. This kind of advertisement allows you to utilize your personal contacts to reach new clients and sell a large order to a group of interested buyers. While network marketing is not a party planning business, sharing your products with a gathered community of friends will help save your time and breath, as you won't have to individually go from person to person to make more than one sale in a day. Hosting events will expand your audience, increase your exposure, and secure new leads and clients for your small business.

- Lead Team Events – Take Your Local Team Out to Social Gatherings

  Once you have established your own small team of workers, they become one of your greatest assets and should be treated as such. You should work to become close to your team members and encourage them to reach out to your social circle and vice versa. You and your team can help build your business through coffee, cocktails and conversation events, customer appreciation celebrations, and vendor events. For example, once a month, reach out to your team, family members, and friends to share product stories, product demonstrations, and fun games to help establish interpersonal connections. Everyone will have a chance to share their success stories and meet new people. This kind of gathering will also relieve any pressure on your inner circle to purchase your products. After spending time with you and your team, they will see how great your services and goods are on their own!

- Make Appearances at Trade Shows and Farmer's Markets

    Trade shows are filled with people looking to make big buys on multiple products and services; so why not take your business somewhere consumers already go to spend money? Trade shows and farmer's markets allow you to reach a lot of people and establish a great reputation with schools, churches, and local business; all of whom will want to do business with you once they see how amazing your products are! Often times, a booth or table at a farmer's market or trade show costs less than a hundred dollars. An opportunity like this also gives you a chance to reach out to your email list and let them know exactly where to find you.

- Have a Gift, Raffle, or Auction Every Chance You Get

    Who doesn't love free products or a chance to win big? Many sales representatives will use their email lists and Facebook pages to get clients excited about the chance to win new products and spread the word about big events through raffles, auctions, and gifts. A great network marketer knows how important it is to get the product into people's hands, even if it means letting a few free samples slide. Because if the product really is that great, the customer will be back for more and will bring their friends too! Start the conversation by giving an exciting opportunity for your clients to talk about!

- Use the Internet to Your Advantage by Making a Website or Blog

    The internet is a great tool for reaching out to clients and establishing new clientele. Websites and blogs are taking the internet by storm, and everyone knows that a simple Google search will lead you to whatever products and services best fit your needs. If a client cannot remember your phone number, address, or wide range of products, they can easily look up your website and gain access to everything they need to make a purchase. Websites will allow you to list all of your products online to sell, while blogs allow you to personally connect with everyone who finds your website. Creating a website is easier than ever before; it may take a few bucks to buy the domain of the site, but many WordPress and similar sources offer free themes and formatting to get your website started. Not to mention that the internet is accessible all over the world. So, not only will your regulars come looking for new products, but people in other countries will come to your site as well! All you need to do is optimize your website so that it appears first on the Google search page when consumers use keywords to research your product.

- Use Social Media to Personally Connect with Customers and Build a Fan Base

    Facebook has become a stomping ground for businesses and network marketing. In just a few clicks, customers can be scrolling through your page, checking out products and inquiring about purchases. Social media allows you to quickly find out what kind of customer base is interested in your business and weed out the people who couldn't care less about what you have to say or sell. People love getting to know the person behind the counter – the face of the product. You can easily make a Facebook page that uses your name with the name of the multi-level marketing company. You can promote your Facebook page in order to get more 'Likes' and use your fan bases to gain interest in products. You should update your page at least every other day with news about your company, products, customer experiences, updates, events, and chances to win products.

- Use Google AdWords to Get Your Business to the Top

    Google AdWords is one of the most effective and efficient methods when you are looking to promote your network marketing business. The process of creating an account and getting started is easy, but you do need a credit card, debit card, or net banking in order to purchase the advertisements. However, once you have created your AdWords account, you can almost immediately post an ad to the first page of Google that is seen by anyone who searches for your potential keywords. This will drive in legitimate traffic to your website and help your network grow much faster. Just using Google AdWords alone can potentially earn you a full-time income.

- Use Pamphlets to Spread Your Message

    Pamphlet distribution is one of the oldest and most effective methods to promote your business. Plus, it is incredibly cheap to do if you are a start-up business that is still trying to get established. Handing out pamphlets is a great way to weed out uninterested consumers and steer the potential clients to your business. The people who do not want your services will throw away the pamphlet, while the interested customers will contact you directly.

- Use Your Local Cable Television Station

    People are always looking for ways to help out small, family-owned businesses, and contribute to making the local economy grow. Just by turning on the television, consumers are able to pinpoint successful local businesses because they advertise on the local cable station. For a reasonable price, you can purchase ad time on your local TV channel and reach a new community of customers.

Enjoying your eBook so far? Take a moment to subscribe to our FREE newsletter for incredible discounts, books giveaways, and VIP offers!

> ➤ http://www.connectionbooksclub.com/bonus/

All we need is your email, and you'll be set up to receive more of the eBooks you can't wait to read.

People Management And Team Building

Now you are an experienced network marketer; you have established your business within the community, your sales are up, and your company is growing rapidly. Now, it is time for you to start recruiting new members to become a part of your team and help the business grow even more. Building a reputable sales team is an exciting new step to become a great network marketer. However, you do not want just anybody to be on your team. Your team will represent the company; they will become the face of the operation and directly interact with customers. Here is how to recruit the right members to be a part of your branch of the company:

1. Make Working for the Company an Enjoyable Experience
    - Your members should represent everything that your business stands for. Network marketing is all about interacting with the local community to establish a reputable presence around town. Therefore, your team should be made up of responsible local faces. With both yours and their inner circles combined, you will be able to promote your business and gain the community's confidence by having people who clients can recognize behind the sales table.
    - Plan an exciting orientation meeting to get your new recruits excited for this amazing opportunity. Plan the day around team building exercises, free snacks, and informative sales exercises to get your team started on the right foot.

2. Give New Recruits the Opportunity to be Recognized by their Friends
    - o Send out welcome letters to all of your new members and potential members. You should also include a new member kit with your welcome letter, which will include:
        - A list of staff and their contact information
        - A publication catalogue or pamphlet of your products and services.
        - A copy of your business's latest newsletter and updates on where the company is at the point in time.
        - An invitation to your next team meeting to introduce them to the rest of the team.
        - A list of upcoming calendar events.
        - A welcome letter from the company's board members.
        - A thank-you note to members already involved in the business's success and recognition of their hard work.
3. Talk to the Potential Recruits About What Opportunities Working for You Will Give Them
    - Make contact with the potential recruits via telephone, postcard, letter, and email.
    - Give them a newsletter or pamphlet about the benefits of working for your company.

- Send out surveys asking customers and members what they want to see happen in the company and how to make their experience even better.
- Have a senior member send out a letter of appreciation and recognition to your new members.

4. Get Your Current Team Members Involved with the Recruitment Process

    - Offer your team members incentives for recruiting new members.
    - Current members are the most relatable people for recruits to talk to. As long as you treat your team with respect and gratitude, their honest opinion about their experience with the company will be enough to convince anyone to join.

Congratulations, you have created a team of elite and capable salesmen ready to dive into network marketing! But now comes the hard part; getting your team to perform well and make sales is the defining factor that determines how successful your business will be. After a few months, your team may start underperforming and you may not know what exactly to do to turn things around. For example, your team members may be constantly arriving late for meetings, not meeting their sales goals, or have lost their drive. Leading a team of sales representatives can be difficult, so here are some of the best tips to help you manage your team and keep them up to par:

- Motivation is a powerful management tool. Employees thrive on inspiration and excitement, which means that you need to be the driving force behind their success. Your job as the employer is to lead by example. You set the precedent for your team and need to demonstrate the right habits and behaviors to present themselves appropriately to customers. Embody the values that represent the company: honesty, integrity, quality, etc.

- Develop emotional intelligence; the ability to understand and manage your own emotions. Emotional intelligence means that you are aware and sensitive to the emotions and psychological needs of the customers and your team members. Individuals who exhibit personal emotional and psychological development have been proven to have improved job satisfaction and a more cohesive sales team. Those who lack this crucial skill are less aware of their emotions and actions, and underperform in their sales goals.

- Focus on building stable and healthy work relationships with your team members. Your team members rely on each other while also being one another's competitors. Establishing good working relationships amongst your team members is vital to the company's success. Healthy relationships promote team morale, productivity, and better collaborations. Strong relationships make it much easier to reach an agreement in group decisions and create opportunities for people to get to know one another.

- Come to know and understand each of your team member's personalities. To properly and efficiently manage your team, you need to be able to recognize and understand each person's strengths and weaknesses. This will not only help your pair strong team members together, but also help you come up with unique motivation and reward strategies. Create a personality profile for each of your team members and use them to assign your people tasks that best fit their strengths.

- Use positive motivation and rewards to keep your team members dedicated to reaching goals and happy to contribute to the sales effort. Your members are individually unique and will be motivated by different things. As the leader of your organization, you need to figure out what motivates your team and find how to use their drive to progress the company. Some forms of motivation may include:

  - Bonus or commission checks
  - Small presents
  - Certification opportunities
  - An extra day off
  - Leadership opportunities

However, as you utilize motivation tactics, be sure that the compensation is appropriate to the situation. But also make sure that the reward is fair and your team members are happy. Talk to each team member privately to learn how they would like to be compensated when they go above and beyond. Knowing there are ways that they can earn a little something extra may drive them to work harder.

Setting S.M.A.R.T. Goals

Goal-setting is essential for a company's success. Goals move you forward in life and fuel your purpose. They outline what you really want in life and put your current circumstances into perspective. Determining how far you want to take your business helps you realize how significant and important setting goals is, especially when your livelihood is at stake. To improve your team's focus, measure their progress, and overcome procrastination, set SMART goals to drive your team's success.

SMART stands for:

- **S**ignificant
- **M**easureable
- **A**ttainable
- **R**ealistic
- **T**imely

SMART goals help narrow your focus and make sales. A great sales team is made up of ambitious and motivated professionals. While many leaders want to focus on the numbers, the real struggle is trying to efficiently manage a sales team. But be sure not to micromanage your workers; setting individual SMART goals for each of your members will help you effectively manage your team while not overstepping your boundaries as their boss.

Finding Motivation And Making The Final Sale

Regardless of how good you are with people, your business will never grow if you do not sell the product. Networking is more than just talking to people; you have to sell the product while building a strong relationship with your customer. To successfully market your products and services, you need to be able to positively influence people into making the purchase – part of what comes with being a good listener. One of the most aggravating traits that marketers exhibit is trying to upsell their products without being aware of the customer's feelings. This is why you hang up the phone every time a telemarketer calls; you know that they will not stop talking and pressuring you to buy into whatever they are selling until you either hang up or give in. Not to mention that a company whose methods are focused on pressuring consumers is a giant red flag indicating a scam.

In a precious chapter, we discussed how practicing empathy is what separates the best salesmen from the mediocre ones. Listening is one of the most important traits that allows you to connect with your customers and show that you really do care about their needs. By listening to your client, you are learning how to correctly market your product or service to show how it fits their wants and needs. You are collecting vital information that will sell your product to each individual customer while making them feel special and heard.

Once you have heard your customer's thoughts and feelings, you need to appropriately convey how your product will improve their life. This is when you use previous customers as examples to influence your client to move forward with the sale. Recounting stories to potential customers of successful, satisfied customers that have purchased your product before will show that you are an honest salesperson who only sells high-quality products that fit the individual needs of each customer. To further the sale, and prove your trustworthy and positive image, go one step further by giving your client your previous customer's contact information.

The customer's experience with you is what sells the product, not how good the product really is. The deciding factors that will influence any consumer to make a purchase are:

- Relatability
- Personalized Customer Service
- Highlighting the Benefit of the Product
- Handwriting Personal Notes and Recommendations
- Use Positive and Appropriate Body Language
- Understanding What the Customer Wants
- Agreeing with the Customer on Something Relatable
- Not Overwhelming Them with Information
- Taking Your Time with Making the Sales

Lastly, and possibly the most crucial step to making a sale, is knowing your product. You should know your services and products better than anyone. You should be able to efficiently, confidently, and completely answer any question your customer asks you. Before going into a sales call, you should already know at least the most basic information about your product. This helps you establish the value of your brand and reassure the customer that your product is legitimate. Before reaching out to consumers, you should know:

- What the purpose of your product or service is
- How to accurately describe your product
- How your customer can access the product and how it will be delivered to him or her
- How much the product costs and why it costs as much as it does
- Any conditions for its use that may impact the product or the customer's experience with it
- Why your product and brand is the best option for the consumer
- How economical or sustainable the product is
- The longevity of the product and how the consumer's environment or location will change the product.

Communication Is Key

In today's modern world, there are dozens of different ways to communicate with one another. There are emails, Facebook messages, tweets, text messages, phone calls, etc. – all of them helping members of society meet each other and come across new information. Along with every new outlet, there is a different device to use. But regardless of how easy it may be to contact someone; the faceless communication has left conversations as impersonal and hastened interactions. Face-to-face communication skills are slowly being pushed aside for virtual contact, and humans are losing basic one-on-one interaction. As a network marketer, it is your job to talk with as many people as possible in order to sell your product. Although social media updates and friendly emails are an easy way to contact large groups of people all at once, it is the face-to-face communication that is going to get you your biggest sales.

Face-to-face upselling is the most effective way to build trust with your customers and make sales. It shows that you care about making that personal contact with your clients and can physically display the quality of your products. We all prefer to work with people that we trust and share common interests with. As you enter into a conversation with a potential client, offer the person a warm smile and a welcoming handshake; this kind of open and friendly body language sets a positive and professional tone.

The overall goal is to have laid down the foundations for a strong relationship; but you need to make an effort first before any kind of relationship can be formed. Start by making light conversation before getting down to business. This will allow you to feel out the customer's mood, understand his or her thoughts, and find something that you both have in common. Your intent listening, sharing of thoughts and ideas, and mutual agreement on something will establish the basis for a relationship. Furthermore, this basic small talk will give you a chance to find out why this person in particular would want or need your product. How can it fit into his or her life? How can it alter or improve their current situation? After you have found a way that the customer can use the product, it is time to start selling.

Begin by asking relevant questions to the person's situation and understanding how your products or services can be useful. This is how you create the opportunity to talk about what you are selling. Explain how the product or service can benefit your customer and even use examples to further your sales pitch. This kind of interaction is incredibly difficult to do over the phone or through email. You can physically keep the customer's interest through body language, eye contact, and tone of voice. Most of the time, people would rather receive a piece of snail mail than have a four-minute conversation over the phone. Face-to-face conversation also allows you to form a recognizable relationship that will make following up with the customer that much easier.

By engaging in real conversation, you are able to establish loyalty and trust with your clients. And just as importantly, you also make sales much faster. It is easy to say a quick 'no' and hang up on a telemarketer. But when you put a face and real live human being with their own story into the picture, it is much harder for a potential customer to throw away their sympathy and tell you to take a hike. Face-to-face conversations allow you to put a face to the voice and a name with the product. The sales pitch is no longer just about the product, but about both yours and the customer's lives, which are priceless. By making physical contact, you are finding out how to tailor your products and services to the person's needs, and this makes their decision much simpler.

One popular product that network marketers over the phone tend to sell is magazines. Even if a customer shows a slight interest in purchasing a few subscriptions, that curiosity is thrown out the door once the sales representative starts rapping through every single product they offer. You would hang up the phone too, if someone needed more than twenty seconds to describe what they are offering. Customers, just like you, want your sales pitch simple and straight to the point. They should not have to answer a dozen questions and fill out a survey to determine if the product is right for them. Your clients already know what they like, want, and need. They do not need an entire slide show documenting all the reasons they should buy your product. No matter who you are trying to sell to, you should be able to tell them exactly why your company has what they need without digressing into a rant. You should offer simple choices of products that balance their needs with the price tag. All of this factors into a "yes" sooner rather than later or never.

Upselling

As a network marketer, your goal is to sell the product. However, simply putting a reasonable price sticker on your goods will not convince the passerby to make that impulsive buy. Upselling, by definition, is a sales method in which the sales representative induces the consumer to buy more expensive items or upgrades in order to make a more profitable sale. A specific technique of upselling known as "point of sale" promotion or impulse buying, will make selling small ticket products ideal at the time of purchase. This practice thrives on the element of placement, rather than the behavior or actions of the sales representative.

For example: if you go online to a clothing retailer's website, you will see that they have their items clearly marked and categorized on the home page's menu. Even more importantly, the very first thing that will pop up as you are initially brought to the site is the most current sale. Right away, the customers are introduced to the best bargains and do not have scroll through the entire site to find what they want. Not only does this bring loyal customers back time and time again, but it will also catch the eye of any person who just happens upon the website.

Here are the four crucial steps to efficiently and effectively upselling your merchandise:

1. Wait

    Wait until your customer has officially decided to make a purchase before offering additional products or services. If you try to strike a deal before they are even committed to a product, then it can come off as too aggressive and intimidating. Do not scare the customer off by trying to upsell another item. Let them take their time making a decision before attempting to add in something else.

2. Collect information

   This goes back to the basic rules and strategies of face-to-face communication. You need to know what a customer is looking for in the first place before trying to sell them a product. You would not try to sell a coffee pot to someone who just wanted a pillow case. Take the opportunity to find out the real benefit they are searching for. Once you understand their true needs, you can find a suitable product and additional merchandise.

3. Be reasonable

   Upselling is adding on an unnecessary but thoughtful product to the customer's purchase. Therefore, you should keep in mind the client's budget when picking out the right upsell product. As a general rule of thumb, products for upsell should not increase the entire purchase by more than twenty- five percent. Or else, the customer may feel like they are making too big of a second purchase and that they are not saving enough money on their end of the bargain.

4. Add value

   This is possibly the most important part of the upselling process: always add value to the customer's purchase. Do not ever upsell just for the sake of making more money or getting rid of back-stocked inventory. Customers know when there is a deal to be had and when a scam is underway. With each upsell, you should have viable reasons why the additional purchase should be considered. If you can identify the value behind an upsell, then so will your customers.

Upselling will benefit any business, no matter the size or the products. By matching up complementary products and creating a sales process that keeps upselling in mind, you can successfully create a way to make additional profits.

Enjoying your eBook so far? Take a moment to subscribe to our FREE newsletter for incredible discounts, books giveaways, and VIP offers!

> ➤ http://www.connectionbooksclub.com/bonus/

All we need is your email, and you'll be set up to receive more of the eBooks you can't wait to read.

Keeping Your Eyes On The Competition

A little competition is healthy for any business, especially when it comes to network marketing. Even if a similar company moves in next door, there is enough room for both of you to exist – for now. Your competing company is quite possibly the biggest asset to your success. Why? Because you can learn from them by studying their tactics, strengths, and weaknesses. If you take a look at the world's most successful people – athletes, entrepreneurs, CEO's, etc. – you will discover that they take the time to study their competition and understand what makes them tick. However, to successfully utilize your competitor's techniques, you need to know exactly what to look for. Because you are not looking to steal their ideas or copy their products; you want their strategies and reasons for using certain methods of selling.

Being a copycat is not the answer to beating your competitors. If you just copy whatever your rival does, you will always be one step behind. However, if you can analyze their moves and understand why they make the decisions they do, then you can spot lucrative opportunities you would have otherwise missed. Start by checking out what other people are saying about your competitors to further product development and improve your own services. How can their failures and successes help you develop your sales tactics and improve? If you see consumers complaining about the quality, usability, or price of your competitor's merchandise, you will be able to pinpoint the areas your own company can do better with. It really is that easy. Your customers know what they want, and if you actively listen and adjust your own business, they will come to you for their needs.

Your competitor's failures should not be the only driving force for changing your sales strategies. A rival's success is just as important because you can learn what *your* business is doing wrong. When you see what your competitor is doing right and hear a customer boast about their experience, you are gaining direct insight to exactly what the customer is looking for. Then, you will be able to cater to that. As long as your similar tactic is better, you will be able to be the number one source for your clients' needs.

Building a Steady Income

You have successfully joined a network marketing business and started making sales. Your progress is rapidly increasing and you have finally begun to make back the money from your initial investment. Now, it is time to up your game and make life-changing strides. Many people take up network marketing as a way to make some extra money while still working a nine-to-five job. But the most successful network marketers are able to efficiently make their marketing career their only source of income. Network marketing can give you the freedom to live out your dreams by granting you personal freedom with your time and financial independence. Why spend the rest of your career punching someone else's clock when you can make your own hours and the potential for unlimited income. You decide how long you want to work and how much effort you put into making sales. Your successes are earned in their own right, while your failures are respective to your persistence and dedication. But with enough motivation, determination, and effort, you can build a steady and livable income with network marketing.

So how do you begin this transition from a full-time job to network marketing? Fortunately, this chapter contains a step-by-step process that will help you every step of the way towards financial freedom. However, you cannot just quit your job on a whim and take a leap of faith into the world of network marketing. You need to have established a stable income for at least six months before you can wave goodbye to your current job.

Step 1: Choose a product line for your network marketing business. For example: nutrition. Nutritional network marketing companies are become more popular by the minute. But as fad diets, obesity, and fast food chains continue to grow, the general population will always need a source for health goods and services.

Step 2: Now that you have found your product idea, search for a wholesale supplier to buy from. The National Association of Wholesaler-Distributors offer many high quality companies to make your purchases from. Just go to Naw.org to have a look at their list of reliable names. You can also sign up for free trade publications at Tradepub.com for more sources.

Step 3: Make contact with several potential wholesale and manufacturer distributors. Inquire about their drop-shipping services and if they offer supplier catalogs and order forms for the products. And of course, choose the distributor that offers you the lowest unit cost per product.

Step 4: Now that you have officially found a supplier, it is time to develop your own sales strategy. You need to set the retail price of your merchandise; but keep in mind that your price should be in accordance with your supplier's sales suggestions. Then, decide upon a commission system for your distributors on a variety of levels. For example, set a commissions at ten percent for first-level representatives, in which a distributor will earn money off of the products your team sells.

Step 5: Make up an instruction manual for your sales representatives and distributors with various ways to advertise your new network marketing company. Also, create a sample kit for your employees to efficiently sell likeable and useable products. This kit should include product samples, instructions, a catalog, prices, and order forms.

Step 6: Start advertising as soon as you have found employees and have physical products to sell. You can contact magazines, newspapers, radio stations, farmer's markets, or even local businesses to support your blossoming company. Utilize all of the methods that were detailed in chapter three.

Step 7: Now is the time to directly contact customers; whether you have purchased a product virtually or in person. If someone responds to your ad, then mail out a personal sales letter, brochure, and order form. If a potential customer calls your business line to find out more information about your services, give them a call back.

Understanding Taxes

Well, you have officially started a successful network marketing career and have made a significant amount of income. However, just like with any other business, there is one looming factor that you have no choice but to face: taxes. Everybody dreads the T word; but as a new business owner and independent marketer, you have to thoroughly study and understand every aspect of filing and recording the taxes of your network marketing business. There are three types of federal business taxes that affect network marketers: income tax, self-employment tax, and employment tax. Almost all of your tax information will be recorded on a 1040 tax form and its succeeding parts, for example: Schedule A for itemized deductions, Schedule C for profit or loss, Schedule C- EZ for net profit, and Schedule SE for self-employment tax.

Employment taxes are only applicable to network marketers who hire employees to work for them. For the specific requirements to determine whether someone who works for you is considered an employee by the United States government, consult the IRS Revenue ruling 87-41 or call 800-TAX-FORM for more information.

Due to the increase in the number of people quitting their jobs to work from home or become self-employed, the IRS had to reevaluate what kind of deductions and breaks to give these new entrepreneurs. In 1999, the IRS allowed home offices to count as deductions in order to make tax planning more appealing to network marketers. Therefore, if your network marketing business is truly your main stream of income, then you can qualify for a few amazing tax advantages that are available to other business owners.

While tax deductions are something to be happy about and look forward to, there is some bad news with network marketing and taxes. There are hundreds of tax codes, regulations, and interpretations that could seriously impact your small business. All of these rules play an important part with your tax filing as a business owner. Therefore, it is crucial that you recognize and understand every detail of your taxes in order to avoid getting into trouble with the IRS. The IRS states that you cannot deduct certain business expenses unless you use the questioned circumstance for business profit, rather than just a hobby. So how do you know how the IRS will view your company? The IRS will use one of two tests to make its decision: the first being whether you have made a profit in three out of five years. The second is if you are able to show them that you purposefully use your business to make a significant profit. In this case, the IRS is looking at whether you treat your business in a professional manner and dedicate the appropriate time and energy into helping it succeed and whether you depend on the income from your business to live.

<u>Meals and Entertainment</u> Network marketing requires you to personally interact with your clients. Sometimes this includes wining and dining them. But not only will you possibly take clients out to eat, you will also need to feed yourself. You will be on the road often trying to recruit new members and sell your product. Dining and entertainment is one expense that the IRS will whittle away at. These deductions are limited to only fifty percent of your food and

entertainment costs. In this case, you should record your meal and entertainment expenses as deduction claims. Not only does this include your receipts, but also documentation of the business discussion at the time, and business relationship (who you ate with).

Home Office Deduction

Fortunately, you are able to include your home office as a deduction to your taxes. However, you must be prepared to demonstrate how you use your office space. Based on the assumption that your home office meets the qualifications, you can deduct a portion of certain expenses that are related to your entire house. This may include your mortgage payments, utility bills, home insurance, and repair. However, the office space must be used regularly and only for your business. You cannot have any other fixed location for your administrative or management activities.

Ordinary Business Expenses

These ordinary expenses are exactly what you would think business expenses entail. You can deduct expenses like: accounting fees, license fees, advertising fees, etc. However, the greatest advantage with your taxes in this case is that your home life and business life can slightly overlap. You can deduct your telephone bills, office supplies, fax machines, computers, cleaning supplies and services, office furniture, and decorations. This is definitely a great opportunity to take advantage of possible tax deductions and improve your business lifestyle.

Travel and Networking

As a network marketer, you need to travel to make contact with distributors, customers, and new recruits. But if you also have a genuine interest in traveling or your spouse likes to travel, then you can use your love of worldly experience to promote your network marketing business. The business travel deduction is one of the greatest benefits for network marketers. However, you have to have clear proof of your travels being business-related – even with your vacation ventures. There is definitely a blurry line when it comes to the legitimacy of your traveling in relation to your network marketing business. For example, in the United States, all of your travel expenses are considered deductible if the trip is primarily for business. But as you travel overseas, you need to separate the travel expenses between business and leisure time.

Of course, as spring rolls around, so does tax season. Now, you have to take time out of your day to fill out forms and figure out exactly what kind of information the IRS needs to know. Nearly every network marketing wholesale distributor agreement acknowledges your status as an independent contractor status, as does the IRS. Due to the IRS recognizing you as a self-employed individual, you will have to pay income tax and self-employment tax. If you make income more than five hundred dollars a year, then you should be making quarterly tax payments. If you make more than six hundred dollars a year or purchase more than five thousand dollars of product, then you will have to fill out a Form 1099. This form will be attached to your Schedule C, along with your tax return. A Schedule C summarizes your income and expense from the network marketing company.

Assets: Computers, Cars, and Capital

When it comes to your assets, you will certainly need to talk to your tax advisor for personal consultation. You will have to make important choices about how to deduct the purchase costs of your computer, accompanying equipment, and cars that are primarily used for your network marketing company. The IRS has relatively flexible and generous limits on how much you can actually count as a business deduction in a given year. However, the expenses of your assets is limited to the income you make from your business. You also have the option to take a depreciation write-off over multiple years for certain business equipment. However, this information can really be determined by your tax advisor.

The costs of your car specifically for your network marketing company are in fact deductible. However, you can only factor these deductions in one of two ways. You can use the IRS's guideline of cents-per-mile, or by itemizing the car's expenses: gas, maintenance, depreciation, repairs, and insurance can all be deducted if applicable. Of course, you must calculate the percentage of your overall car usage in relation to your network marketing company and adjust the recording of those expenses appropriately.

Most importantly, when it comes to your network marketing business and taxes, you absolutely need to keep detailed recordings of your expenses. If you have the opportunity to talk to the delightful members of the IRS, they will tell you that keeping adequate records of your deductions will help solidify your claims. As your business expenses are the only deductibles you can claim on your taxes, you should look into opening a separate bank account just for these expenses.

You need to also keep a record of every business transaction and retain those records. Receipts in this case, are the best evidence to prove your business expenses.

Enjoying your eBook so far? Take a moment to subscribe to our FREE newsletter for incredible discounts, books giveaways, and VIP offers!

> ➢ http://www.connectionbooksclub.com/bonus/

All we need is your email, and you'll be set up to receive more of the eBooks you can't wait to read.

The Importance of Mentors

Mentors are the most influential people that you can have in your life. Mentors inspire you to set higher goals and motivate you to become a better person, business owner, and leader. In fact, whether or not your mentor is an actual friend of yours, he or she can be the most valuable resource in your journey to financial freedom and self-sustainability. The thought of launching your own business or redirecting your career can be scary and intimidating. You never truly know how this experience will play out and must compete against other local entrepreneurs to make your business stand out. A strong and intelligent mentor can help you avoid pitfalls and teach you how to grow your business at a faster rate.

If you just do a simple Google search, you will immediately find a hundred names of successful business owners willing to share their knowledge of business and communication to help others succeed in achieving their dreams. There are inspirational men and women who come from all fields of the business world, but they each have their own fair share of valid advice to help any business grow. Just because you personally have chosen network marketing as your source of income does not mean that investors, technology developers, or magazine editors do not have anything of value for you to use. Do your own research and find out who is the best person to be your role model based on your personal and business goals.

15. Known Network Marketing Businesses

- Mary Kay Cosmetics- http://www.marykay.com/
- Forever Living –
- http://foreverliving.com/?store=USA&language=en&distribID=001002554163&joinNowPopup
- Amway- http://www.amway.com/
- Avon- https://www2.youravon.com/REPSuite/become_a_rep.page?p=TMI_GGL_SEM_EN_BR&c=c&s=_e_kwid_2016_11152
- Legal Shield- https://www.legalshield.com/personal?gclid=CKS_n7LHs84CFQtZhgodzU0LKw
- Usborne- http://www.theusbornebookstore.com/
- Herbal Life Nutrition- http://www.herbalife.com/
- Youngevity- http://youngevity.com/
- Tupperware- http://www.tupperware.com/
- Scentsy- https://scentsy.com/
- Usana- https://www.usana.com/
- Pampered Chef- https://www.pamperedchef.com/
- Melaleuca - https://www.melaleuca.com/
- Beachbody - https://www.beachbody.com/?e=mm56400
- Jeunesse- https://www.jeunesseglobal.com/

Let's Get Started!

Now that you know the basics of network marketing, you can finally start earning a steady income from your new business. You most likely have a certain image in your mind of what network marketing is all about. But if you really take this business seriously, then you need to realize that network marketing is not just a hobby, it is a legitimate job. You can potentially earn a full-time livable, and sustainable income. But what exactly does it take to succeed in the network marketing industry? Well, there are six key factors that you need to take into serious consideration when starting out with this business.

1. Stability- How old is this network marketing company? Does the company have a long history with loyal customers?

2. Product Quality- How good are the products or services? What is the quality of the products and are the customers' needs met?

3. The Pay Plan- How much is the pay in regards to your effort and the cost of distribution? Is it fair, overpriced, or reasonably cheap? This will determine how you will be paid. Take into consideration: how many pennies out of each sales dollar does the distributors get back each month?

4. Integrity- How is the integrity and the management style of the company? Just like any other serious investment, you should take the time to research the experience of the CEO or person in charge, their own

experience in network marketing, and their career background. Do the people in charge have a good reputation?

5. Timing- Where is the company at in this particular point in time? What is really going on inside the company? Is the company growing or becoming better?

6. The Systems- How are the support, training, and business systems? The company may manage its employees respectfully, have a fair pay plan, and is motivated and growing. However, if their basic support systems are not sufficient, then no other element matters. Proper training is a good indicator of the legitimacy of the company, which is what really counts when you want to invest your livelihood into a new opportunity.

Also take into consideration...

- Does the company practice what they teach? In order to be a successful businessman, you have to be able and willing to listen and learn from mentors and more experienced people in the business. The legitimate network marketing businesses in this industry are structured to keep the best interests of the company's veterans aligned with new recruits'. The systems that are placed within the company will tell you what the boss's values are and whether they are honest and customer-driven.

- How are the higher-ups treated and how do they treat you? The people above you in the chain of command will determine your place in the company. Therefore, you should consider how they take to you professionally and on a personal basis. Are they supportive of your success? How do they treat you in the office? Do they help you with your business management and offer advice? Are they as committed to your success as you would want them to be? Your higher-ups should be relatable and be ready and willing to listen to your troubles with advice to offer.

- The people below you are just as important as the mentors above. A common term in the network marketing business is "orphans"- as in people who are brought in by someone of your status or higher, and then are pushed to the side by them because the person is too busy with other responsibilities. You should take some of these lost recruits under your wing and spend quality time with them. If you have to, then you should train them, support them, and boost their confidence when needed. But the question you really need to consider is: are you willing and ready to be some else's mentor? Being another person's mentor is a great way to build relationships within the workplace.

- Can you and the company efficiently and successfully take care of business? Network marketing is a business, and it should run just as smoothly as a storefront or franchise. Therefore, you should have a reliable and trustworthy accountant to help you along the way. It is very important that you benefit from all of the same tax write-offs as any other full-time business. You should also do as much research as possible before you start making money from your company. Your accountant will be just one member of your strong support team. You should also look into what kind of lawyers to hire and how they can help your business succeed by understanding how certain laws affect your business.

- Are you ready to get rid of your day job just yet? Do not quit your job until you are one hundred percent certain that the money you are making from network marketing is steady, sustainable, and reliable. Make sure that you have been with the company long enough to know how stable it is and that your income will be greater or at least equal to what you are earning from your day job.

Dear Reader,

Connection Books Club wants to thank you for the purchase of one of our many informative eBooks! We hope you enjoyed your purchase and we want to invite you to join our club.

When you subscribe to our FREE club, you'll receive regular newsletters and incredible discounts on our bestselling books! Connection Books Club makes reading easy, giving you the content you want, at a price you can't believe. All that it takes to enroll in our FREE book club is your email. We'll send you the latest business and personal development news and highlight the newest books that are ready for you to enjoy.

http://www.connectionbooksclub.com/bonus/

As part of your subscription, we're giving you a FREE download of one of our favorite eBooks, *Money Management: Learn How to Organize Your Financial Life and Invest in Your Future*. This eBook covers many financial situations, such as lowering interest rates and exploring options surrounding bankruptcy, helping you determine the best financial action for you.

Money management may be difficult for some people, but with your FREE copy of *Money Management: Learn How to Organize Your Financial Life and Invest in Your Future,* you'll learn the skills and information you need to make the best decisions to secure your financial future. The strategies contained in this eBook, designed for the everyday person, offering easy to follow steps and money saving tips.

Understanding money and how to make it works for you is important and with this eBook, you'll learn what you need to know to start building your financial security. Here are the top 5 reasons for reading *Money Management: Learn How to Organize Your Financial Life and Invest in Your Future*:

The strategies in this book are designed to help real people achieve their financial goals.

Explore different options for retirement.

Discover hacks for navigating the grocery store's subtle spending traps.

Inform yourself about how you might be able to get away with paying less than you owe on credit cards and other outstanding debts.

Experience a feeling of newfound freedom when you understand that you have every ability to live a life of financial stability.

Get your copy here: http://www.connectionbooksclub.com/bonus/

The benefits of receiving this eBook for FREE are endless! Take control of your finances and start living the life you want.

By subscribing to Connection Books Club, not only will you get incredible discounts, our FREE welcome gift eBook, and a regular newsletter, but you'll also get the opportunity to receive FREE eBooks! Subscribers are invited to share reviews of the eBooks they've read, earning new titles at no cost! All it takes to enroll is your email. http://www.connectionbooksclub.com/bonus/

Discounts and free eBooks are just a click away! Enter your email for VIP access to new books, incredible deals and money saving options, and even free giveaways! And don't forget, by signing up today for Connection Books Club, you'll receive the incredible eBook *Money Management: Learn How to Organize Your Financial Life and Invest in Your Future* for FREE!

Connection Books Club is excited to have you join our ranks of subscribers. We hope you enjoy your FREE eBook and all the great reading coming your way soon!

http://www.connectionbooksclub.com/bonus/

Conclusion

Thank you again for downloading Network Marketing: A Beginner's Guide for a Successful Network Marketing Career

I hope this book was able to help you to completely understand the workings of a legitimate network marketing business and how you can become a successful sales representative right now! Thousands of people make a livable income through network marketing – and you can too! The next step is to continue doing your own investigation and furthering your research until you are ready to dive into the world of network marketing. You can have a successful and stable self-employed career without sacrificing valuable time with your loved ones. Network marketing may just be the answer to all of your financial and personal needs!

If you've enjoyed this book, I'd greatly appreciate if you could leave an honest review on Amazon.

Reviews are very important to us authors, and it only takes a minute to post

Thank you and good luck!

www.ingramcontent.com/pod-product-compliance
Lightning Source LLC
Chambersburg PA
CBHW060418190526
45169CB00002B/957